P9-DCP-234

DISCARD

Kearsarge Reg. Elem. School Library

New London, N.H.

A New True Book

ANIMALS OF SEA AND SHORE

By Illa Podendorf

This "true book" was prepared
under the direction of
Illa Podendorf,
formerly with the Laboratory School,
University of Chicago

CP CHILDRENS PRESS ™

CHICAGO

Kearsarge Reg. Elem. School Library

New London, N.H.

Collection of Florida
sea shells

PHOTO CREDITS

Lynn M. Stone—2, 17 (4 photos), 19, 20, 23 (2 photos), 24 (right), 31 (right), 32, 33, 36, 41, 42 (bottom)

James P. Rowan—4 (bottom), 6 (right), 11 (top), 16, 24 (left), 31 (left), 39

Louise T. Lunak—4 (top), 42 (top), 45

Allan Roberts—6 (left), 11 (middle & bottom), 12, 15, 21, 26, 28, 30, 34, 35, 38

Marine Mammal Fund:
ᶜ 1980 Lloyd Parker, 8
ᶜ 1979 Blue Whale Expedition, 9
ᶜ Stan Minasian, 18

Joseph A. DiChello, Jr.—13

Julie O'Neil—29

Bill Thomas Photo—Cover, 42 (middle)

COVER—Walruses

Library of Congress Cataloging in Publication Data

Podendorf, Illa.
    Animals of sea and shore.

    (A New true book)
    Revised edition of: The true book of
animals of sea and shore. 1958.
    Summary: Introduces creatures that inhabit
the sea and seashore: animals with fur or
shells, fins or legs, spiny skins or soft
bodies
    1.   Marine fauna—Juvenile literature.
[1.   Marine animals   2.   Seashore biology]
I.   Title.
QL122.2.P63   1982   591.92   81-38453
ISBN 0-516-01615-6   AACR2

Copyright ᶜ 1982 by Regensteiner Publishing Enterprises, Inc.
All rights reserved. Published simultaneously in Canada.
Printed in the United States of America.
Original copyright ᶜ 1958 by Childrens Press.
          7 8 9 10 R 91 90 89 88 87

TABLE OF CONTENTS

Animals with Fur. . . 5

Animals with Fins. . . 10

Animals with Many Legs. . . 13

Animals with Shells. . . 20

Animals with Spiny Skins. . . 29

Animals with Soft Bodies. . . 35

Things to Remember. . . 43

Words You Should Know. . . 46

Index. . . 47

Northern fur seals, Pribilof Islands, Alaska

An elephant seal at a reserve in California

ANIMALS WITH FUR

A seal is a sea animal with fur. It can swim very well. A northern fur seal spends most of its life in the sea. It may stay at sea for six or eight months at one time. It can swim underwater. But it must come to the surface to breathe.

Above:Olga, the walrus at Brookfield Zoo, near
        Chicago
Left:California sea lion, sunning itself in the
        early morning

Sea lions and walruses are relatives of seals.

Whales are relatives of seals, sea lions, and walruses, but they do not have as much fur. In fact, whales have only a little fur, or hair, near their noses.

However, whales are more like their relatives in other ways. A whale baby grows inside the body of its mother. After the baby is born, it drinks milk from its mother's body.

An animal that drinks its mother's milk is called a mammal. Dogs, cats, whales, seals, and human beings are all mammals.

Whales live in the water all the time. When they go under the water, they must hold their breath. They must come to the surface to breathe and to push air out of their lungs.

Blue whale blowing

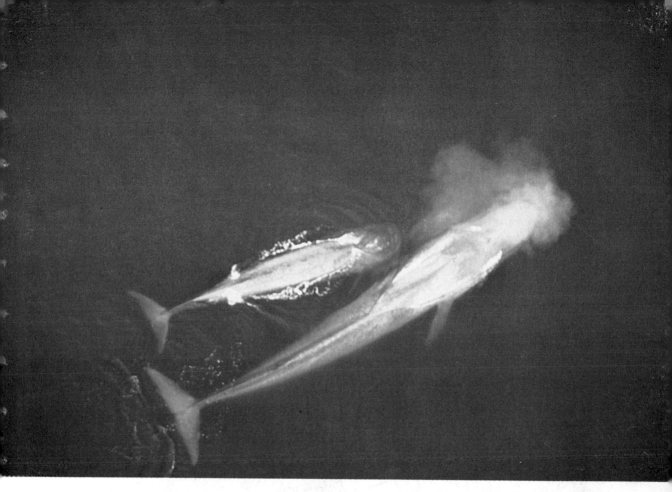

Blue whale and baby

The blue whale is the biggest animal in the world. It is as big as twenty elephants.

ANIMALS WITH FINS

Fish have fins instead of arms and legs. They have gills instead of lungs. Because of their gills, fish are able to breathe under the water. Fish have hard scales on their bodies.

Many fish live in the sea. People and other animals eat fish.

Some fish are strange looking.

Green
moray eel

Triggerfish
among coral

Common
toadfish

Some sea horses are only two inches long. Others may be almost eight inches long.

Sea horses have fins and gills.

The father sea horse has a pouch on the underside of his body. The mother sea horse puts her eggs into this pouch. The father protects the eggs until they hatch.

Live lobsters are dark green, with a little red and blue on them. When cooked, lobsters turn bright red.

ANIMALS WITH MANY LEGS

A lobster has ten legs.
Eight legs are for walking.
Two other legs stick out
and end in large claws.

A lobster has a hard
shell covering its body.
When the lobster grows
too big for the shell, the
shell splits and the lobster
crawls out. The new shell,
which grew under the old
one, is soft at first. But it
soon becomes hard.

Banded coral shrimp

The shrimp has ten legs, but it does not have claws. Shrimp live on the sandy bottom of the sea. They use their fanlike tails to swim backward.

The hermit crab lives in the shell left by another animal. As the crab grows, it must move into a bigger shell.

Crabs also have ten legs. Two of these legs have claws on the end. Crabs can walk forward, backward, and sideways.

There are many kinds of crabs. Some crabs live in burrows on the sandy shore. Other kinds live only in the water.

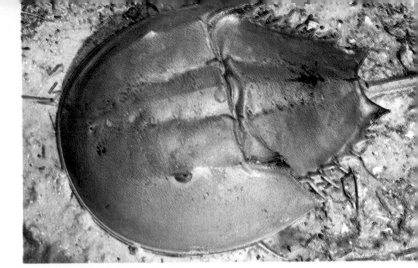

Above: Horseshoe crab
Left: Horseshoe crab
    on its back
Below left: Blue crab
Below right: Fiddler
    crab

Gray whale
covered with
barnacles

Adult barnacles fasten themselves to rocks, ships, and even to other animals. Once a barnacle attaches itself to something, it will spend the rest of its life there. Then a hard shell grows around the barnacle.

Acorn barnacles stay in their shells when the rocks they live on are not covered with water. When the water covers the rocks, the barnacles put out their many feet and kick food into their mouths.

Barnacles on old wood

ANIMALS WITH SHELLS

Oysters have two shells. These shells protect their soft bodies. The shells are held together on one side by a hinge.

Oysters

These oyster shells show how the common oysters
grow together in the sea.

Very young oysters swim
about. Grown-up oysters
attach themselves to rocks
or other things at the
bottom of the ocean. They
feed on tiny plants and
animals in the water.

Oysters lay millions of eggs each year. However, few oysters live for very long because the oyster has many enemies. People catch and eat millions of oysters every year.

Scallops also have two shells. Scallops swim by opening and closing their shells. As the water is forced out, the scallop is pushed along.

Above: Steamer clams
Left: A quahog is a
    thick-shelled clam.

Clams have two-piece shells, too. There are two kinds of clams. One kind has a hard shell and the other has a soft shell.

Above: Scorpion conch
Right: Crown conch

A conch has one hard, spiral shell. Conch shells may be of many different colors.

The conch has one large foot. It uses this foot to move over the ocean bottom.

The squid and the octopus are related to the oyster, clam, scallop, and conch. But they look quite different. All of these animals are called mollusks. They all have soft bodies, without bones. Some, like the oyster, have a hard outer shell. The squid has a shell inside its body. The octopus has no shell at all.

Some squids are very big. Some are small enough
to be held in a hand.

A squid is long and thin.
It swims by forcing water
through a tube under its
head. Because the water
comes out toward the
front, the squid moves
backward.

Squids have ten arms.
Two of their arms are
longer than the others.
Each arm has suckers with
which the squid catches
its food. Squids protect
themselves by shooting a
dark liquid into the water.
It hides them from their
enemies.

Octopus

The octopus lives in caves or among rocks at the bottom of the sea. It swims by forcing water out of a tube under its head. The octopus has eight arms, called tentacles. It uses these arms to pull itself along and to catch food.

Starfish

ANIMALS WITH SPINY SKINS

A starfish is not a fish. It is a member of a group of animals with spiny skins.

Most kinds of starfish have five arms, but some have more. A basket starfish has many arms.

Close-up
of the
tube feet of
a starfish

If a starfish loses an arm, a new one will grow in its place. If a starfish is cut in half, each half will become a new starfish.

Each starfish arm is lined with tube feet. At the end of each tube foot is a sucker. This sucker helps the starfish to crawl and to get its food.

The starfish's mouth is located on the underside of the middle part. It leads straight into the stomach. The starfish is able to push its stomach out through its mouth.

A sea urchin also has a spiny skin and tube feet with strong suckers.

Rock-boring urchin

Sea urchin's empty shell

Empty
sand
dollars
on a
beach

Sand dollars and sea cucumbers have tube feet and spiny skins, too.

A sand dollar lives on the bottom of the sea.

An empty sand dollar shell does not look like the live sand dollar. When it is alive, the sand dollar is purple.

Sea cucumber

Sea cucumbers protect
themselves in a strange
way. They throw sticky
threads out of their
mouths. Their enemies get
caught in the threads. This
gives the sea cucumber
time to get away.

Fossil of sea lilies

Sea lilies look like plants, but they are animals. In fact, they are relatives of the starfish and the sea cucumber.

The sea lily has arms that wave like feathers. It has a foot at the end of each long stalk.

Jellyfish

ANIMALS WITH
SOFT BODIES

Jellyfish is the popular
name for a sea animal
that is not a fish.
Scientists call this animal
a medusa.

35

In the water a moon jellyfish looks like an umbrella with fringe. But when it is out of water, it has no shape. It looks like jelly.

Jellyfish catch their food by stinging it. The sting of the jellyfish can be painful.

Floating jellyfish

The Portuguese man-of-war is a kind of jellyfish. Because of its bag full of gas it is able to float on the water. Its tentacles may be a hundred feet long. The tentacles are used to catch food. They are used for protection, too. They contain a poison. Anyone touching them will get a painful shock.

The polyp is a relative of the jellyfish and the sea anemone.

The tiny polyp forms a covering of lime around itself. Coral, a limestone, is made from the skeletons of millions of these tiny animals.

There are many kinds of coral.

Coral

Sea anemone

Sea anemones are
animals, too. They are
much bigger than coral
animals. They do not form
a hard covering around
themselves. They are able
to move, but usually stay
in one place.

Sea anemones use their tentacles to catch food. If a fish swims too near, the sea anemone reaches out and stings it with its poison tentacles. Then it pulls the fish into its mouth. Its mouth is in the middle of its body.

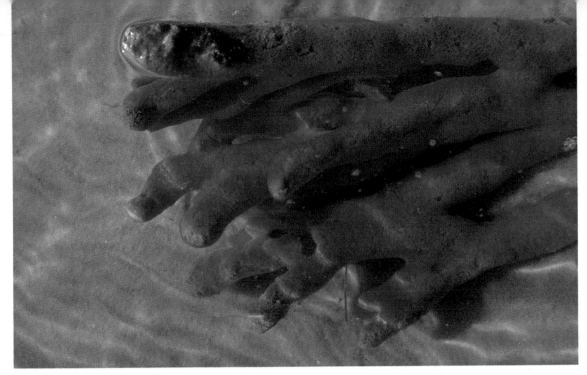

A sponge called dead man's fingers

A sponge is an animal.
Sponges may be black,
brown, yellow, red, blue, or
purple.
Like the starfish, a
sponge is able to grow
from a piece of itself.

Sally Lightfoot
crabs

Close-up of a
baby elephant
seal

Starfish

THINGS TO REMEMBER

Many different kinds of animals live in the sea. Some spend all their lives in the water. Some live on the land part of the time.

Some sea animals have fur or hair on their bodies. Some are covered with scales. Still others have hard shells covering them.

Sea animals with gills
can breathe underwater.
Sea animals with lungs
must come to the surface
to breathe.

Fish have fins, scales on
their bodies, and gills
instead of lungs. Gills
make it possible for fish to
breathe underwater.

Great gray whale

Whales are mammals. They must come to the surface to breathe.

All sea animals are important. Each one gives the sea and its shores something special.

WORDS YOU SHOULD KNOW

antenna(an • TEN • uh) — long, thin feelers on the head of some animals

burrow(BURR • oh) — a hole or tunnel dug in the ground by some animals

disk — thin, flat round object

fringe(FRINJ) — an edge made of hanging things

gills — the body part used for breathing by fish and other animals

hinge(HINJ) — a joint

lung — the body part of mammals used in breathing

mammal(MAM • uhl) — a group of animals that have hair or fur on their bodies, and have young that drink their mother's milk. The word mammal comes from the name of the gland that produces the milk.

medusa(muh • DOO • suh) — a type of a jellyfish

mollusk(MAHL • usk) — a group of animals that have a soft body usually live in water.

polyp(PAHL • ip) — a small water animal with a tube-shaped body

pouch(POWCH) — part of an animal's body that is like a bag or pocket

scale(SKALE) — a small, thin part that forms the skin of fish and reptiles

spiral(SPY • rul) — a curve that widens as it goes around

spout — to send out liquid in a steady stream

stalk(STAWK) — the part of the body that connects an animal to an object

tentacle(TEN • tuh • kil) — the thin arm that comes out from the body of some animals

INDEX

anemones, sea, 38, 39, 40
arms, starfish, 29, 30
baby whales, 7
barnacles, 18, 19
basket starfish, 29
blue whale, 9
breathing, whales, 8
cats, 7
clams, 23, 25
claws, conch, 24
claws, crabs, 16
claws, lobster, 13
conch, 24, 25
coral, 38
crabs, 16
cucumbers, sea, 32, 33, 34
dogs, 7
dollars, sand, 32
fins, animals with, 10-12, 44
fish, 5, 10, 40, 44
fur, animals with, 5-9, 43
gills, 10, 12, 44
human beings, 7
jellyfish, 35-37, 38
legs, animals with many, 13-19
lilies, sea, 34
limestone, 38
lobsters, 13, 14
lungs, 8, 10, 44
mammals, 7, 45
medusa, 35
mollusks, 25

moon jellyfish, 36
northern fur seals, 5
octopus, 25, 28
oysters, 20-22, 25
polyp, 38
Portuguese man-of-war, 37
sand dollars, 32
scales, 10, 43, 44
scallops, 22, 25
sea anemones, 38, 39, 40
sea cucumbers, 32, 33, 34
sea horses, 12
sea lilies, 34
sea lions, 6
sea urchins, 31
seals, 5, 6, 7
shells, animals with, 14, 18, 19, 20-27, 43
shrimp, 15
soft bodies, animals with, 35-41
spiny skins, animals with, 29-34
sponges, 41
squids, 25-27
starfish, 29-31, 34, 41
tentacles, octopus, 28
tentacles, Portuguese man-of-war, 37
tentacles, sea anemones, 40
tube feet, 30, 31, 32
urchins, sea, 31
walruses, 6
whales, 6-9, 45

About the author

Born and raised in western Iowa, Illa Podendorf has had experience teaching science at both elementary and high school levels. For many years she served as head of the Science Department, Laboratory School, University of Chicago and is currently consultant on the series of True Books and author of many of them. A pioneer in creative teaching, she has been especially successful in working with the gifted child.

DATE DUE

NOV 23			
DEC 9			
DEC 22			
JAN 12			
JAN 19			
FEB 13			
Croteau			
NOV 2 1			
2 M			
FEB 1 , 1992			

repaired 7/01:

591.92   Podendorf, Illa
POD   Animals of the sea and shore

Elem. School Library

New London, N.H.